The Bible Beautiful Series

The News about JESUS and How He Saved the World

Written and illustrated
by Benjamin Morse

Published in the United States
under licensed agreement with

ORSON & CO

New York, NY.

www.biblebeautiful.com

ISBN 978-0-9858135-2-9

8 7 6 5 4 3 2 1

This book is about a man who came from heaven.

His name was Jesus, and he was the Son of God.

Jesus made the headlines for the many miracles he performed,

including saving us all from sin and granting us everlasting life.

Matthew

Mark

The news about Jesus was first reported by four evangelists named Matthew, Mark, Luke and John. They each tell their own version of his life and death and do not always agree on the facts.

So these gospel writers are represented by four distinctive symbols: the angel, the lion, the ox and the eagle.

Luke

John

Following their lead, the messengers of Jesus wandered

the ancient world

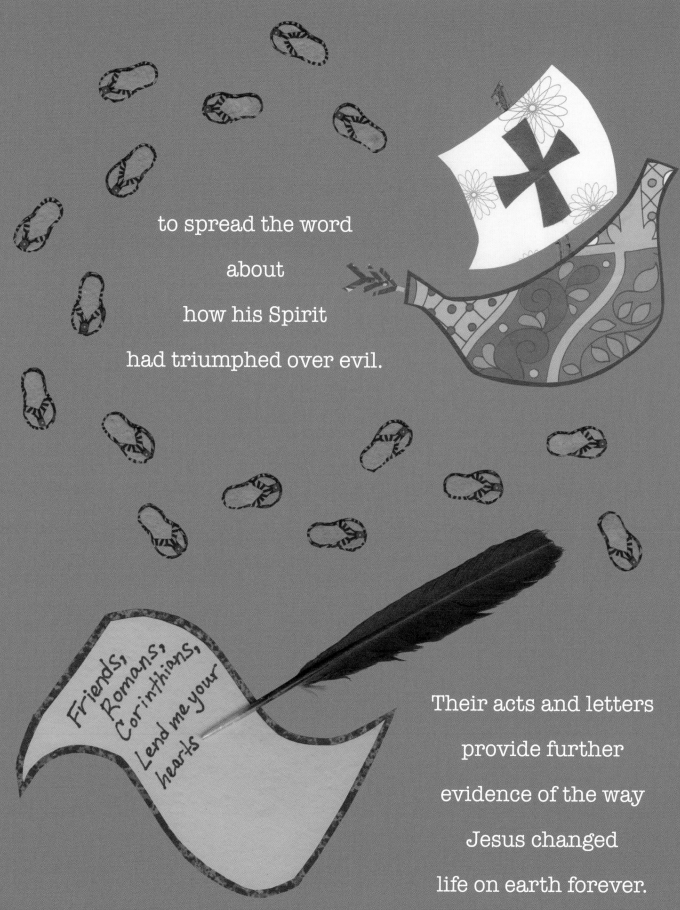

to spread the word

about

how his Spirit

had triumphed over evil.

Friends,
Romans,
Corinthians,
Lend me your
hearts

Their acts and letters

provide further

evidence of the way

Jesus changed

life on earth forever.

A star is born

The story of Jesus begins over 2,000 years ago,

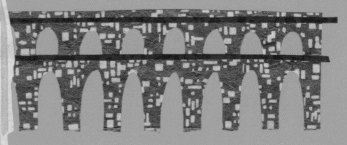

when Augustus Caesar ruled the Roman Empire.

God saw how human power could cause misery and strife and came up with a plan to bring people light and hope.

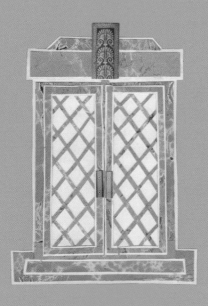

So he sent his angel Gabriel to speak with a Jewish priest named Zechariah in the temple of Jerusalem.

Gabriel told Zechariah
that his elderly wife
Elizabeth
would give
birth to a son
and call him John.

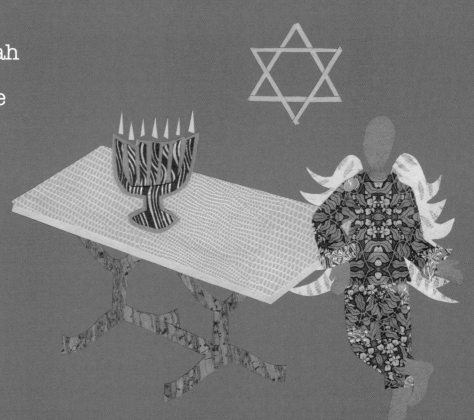

John would clear the way
for the coming of God's own son.

Zechariah was struck dumb by the news.

6

Six months later, Gabriel visited a young relative of Elizabeth's,

a maiden named Mary.

She lived up north in Galilee, in a town called Nazareth.

The angel announced that Mary too would have a son

and call him Jesus.

According to Luke, Mary did not yet have a husband,

so she was especially shocked to hear this.

But Gabriel calmed her down
by promising that the
Holy Spirit would be
the father of her child.

Jesus would be the Son of God.

Mary accepted the angel's word,

declared herself the handmaid of the Lord,
and went to stay with Elizabeth in Judah for a few months.

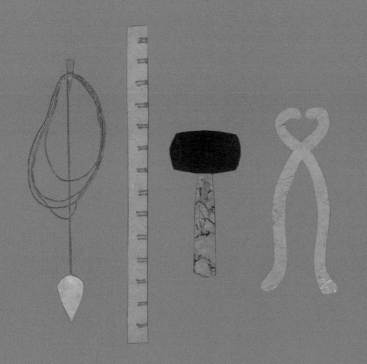

By this time Mary had become engaged to a carpenter named Joseph.

Now when Joseph heard that Mary was pregnant, he wanted to put a stop to the marriage.

But an angel came to him in a dream and told him that the child was from the Holy Spirit, and not another man.

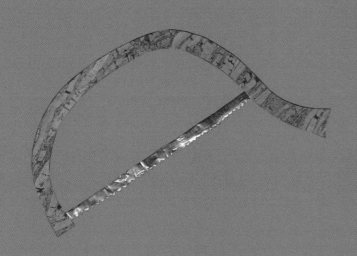

So Joseph became the proud husband of Mary.

When Mary was ready to give birth, Augustus Caesar ordered
a census to be taken.

Everyone had to be recorded
in their hometowns.
So Joseph took Mary
to Bethlehem,
where his ancestor
King David had grown up.

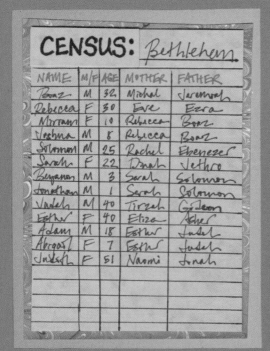

The problem was that Joseph no longer had
any family or friends in Bethlehem.
They tried to check into an inn, but all the rooms were booked.

So Jesus was born in the stable,
which was the last place his parents
expected the Son of God to be born.

His first bed was a manger,
where the animals ate their hay.

That night some shepherds were watching their flock,
when an angel
appeared before them.

They were
positively terrified,
until the angel told them
the joyful news

that Christ the Lord had been born in the city of David.

Then a host of angels filled the sky singing,

"Glory to God in the highest!

Peace will prevail for those

with whom God is pleased!"

The shepherds went in search of the babe
in the manger and told everyone thereafter what they had seen.

Back in Jerusalem, three wise men from the east arrived at the court of King Herod. They had seen a star that meant the king of the Jews had been born.

Herod did not like the sound of this, because he was the official king of the Jews under the Romans. So he sent the wise men to find this so-called Christ and report back to him.

The wise men followed the star to Bethlehem,

where they bowed down and worshipped the newborn.

Then they left him gifts fit for a royal.

KING'S
Quality
Gold
Baby's rattle

Scent of the Stars
Finest
Fabulous
FRANKINCENSE

Myrrh
OF ARABIA
Distinctive aroma
Heals wounds

When the wise men failed to tell Herod that they had found Jesus,
he decreed that all boys recently born in Bethlehem be killed.

Mary and Joseph escaped
with their son to Egypt and
only went to live in Galilee
after Herod died.

All these events fulfilled the
prophecies of ancient Israel.
Little by little, people began to hear that the Messiah had come.

Holy boyhood to baptism

Mary and Joseph did all the things Jewish parents did

to ensure that Jesus would be a child of God.

They had him circumcised and brought him to the Temple in

Jerusalem, where they made sacrifices in thanks for their son.

A man named Simeon

saw this and declared that

the Christ child would bring

salvation to all peoples.

Jesus would not just save Jews, but Gentiles as well.

Every year his parents took him from Nazareth to Jerusalem
for the Passover festival. But one year he gave them quite a fright.
Instead of returning home with them, he stayed in the Temple.

There they found him questioning the teachers about Jewish law.
No one could believe a twelve-year-old could be so curious,
or that he could come up with so many wise answers himself.

In accordance with God's plan, Elizabeth and Zechariah's son
John grew up, and so did Jesus.
John went into the wilderness preaching repentance

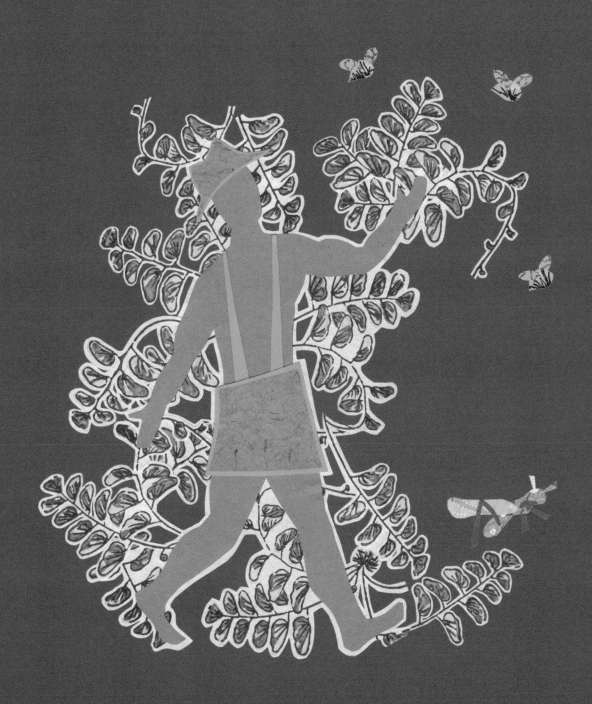

and baptizing people in the River Jordan.

The Old Testament prophet Isaiah had predicted someone would

clear the way for the Lord, and John the Baptist was this man.

One day Jesus himself arrived from Nazareth to be baptized.

John immediately understood
the significance
of his coming.

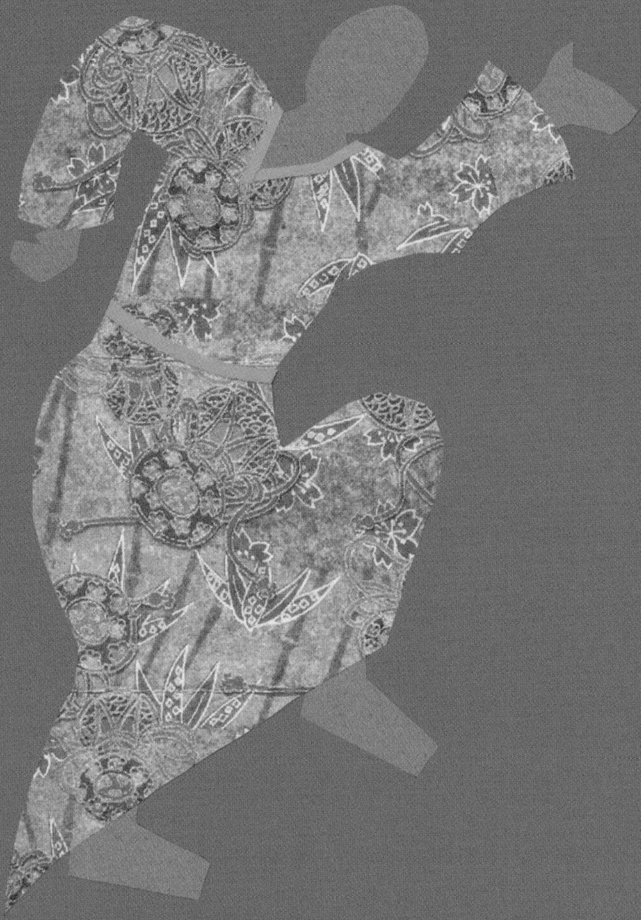

The moment John

cleansed him

with the

waters

of the Jordan,
the heavens opened.

God's own Spirit then came down in the form of a dove and
settled on Jesus. A voice from heaven told him,
"You are my beloved Son,
with whom I am well pleased."

The voice of God told the people that from then on
Jesus would baptize them with the Holy Spirit.

Many people
were confused
by these events.

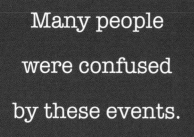

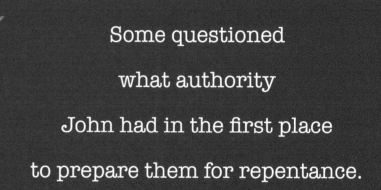

Some questioned
what authority
John had in the first place
to prepare them for repentance.

So John was thrown into prison.

Early career

Jesus meanwhile had fled

to the wilderness

to avoid the attention he was getting

and to think about

what God wanted him to do.

There he fasted for forty days and forty nights.

Jesus was naturally very hungry by the end of this.

The devil came and attempted to trick him,

saying that if

Jesus was the Son of God

then he ought to be able

to turn stones into bread

and feed himself.

But Jesus knew the devil was trying to tempt

him away from God and faithfully replied,

"Man shall not live by bread alone."

When Jesus returned to Galilee, he began preaching

in the synagogues.

Many people praised him,

but his approach to Scripture

and insistence

that the kingdom of heaven was close at hand

caused controversy among the leaders.

So he was expelled from his hometown of Nazareth.

25

From there Jesus went to the Sea of Galilee, where he met several fishermen.

The first two

were brothers:

Simon,

whom Jesus renamed Peter,

and Andrew.

The next two

were also brothers:

James and John,

the sons of Zebedee.

When they decided to follow Jesus,

these disciples became

fishers of men, bringing people on board the boat to salvation.

As they went on their way, eight more
men became disciples of Jesus:

Philip, the patron

saint of bakers,

Nathanael (a.k.a.

Bartholomew),

Matthew (a tax collector

formerly known as Levi),

Thomas

(a.k.a. Didymus),

James the son of

Alphaeus,

Thaddeus

(a.k.a. Jude),

Simon

the Zealot,

and Judas Iscariot.

Soon Jesus began
healing the sick and
casting out demons
from the bodies
they plagued.

He cured Simon-Peter's
mother-in-law
of her fever.

He gave people
who were paralyzed
the ability
to walk again.

He even brought people
back from the dead.

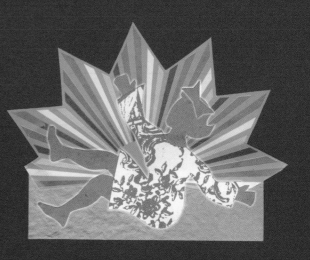

In those days, doctors thought someone could catch leprosy

simply by touching people infected with it,

and that such a sickness made you unholy.

So Jesus shocked everyone when he laid his hands on a man

with leprosy and removed the disease from his body.

At a wedding
in a town called Cana,
there was no wine
to honor the occasion.

So the servants filled

six stone jars with water,

and Jesus turned

the water

into

wine.

He did not
always want
people to publicize such events,
but the news of these miracles spread throughout the land.

Creating a name for himself

Around this time, Jesus made a most inspiring speech.
He challenged the idea that material rewards were
the only sign of God's blessing.

And he promised that
those who were sad or had
been told they were wretched
would find happiness in heaven.

He also told the people not to worry about having fancy clothes.

Like the lilies of the field, which were more beautiful than

anything King Solomon

had ever worn,

God would clothe them.

After all, he added,

it was easier

for a camel to go through the eye of a needle

than for a rich man to go to heaven.

Above everything, Jesus wanted people to honor God and the Commandments by loving their neighbors as themselves.

This meant they should not judge or condemn one another, which he knew even the most religious people liked to do.

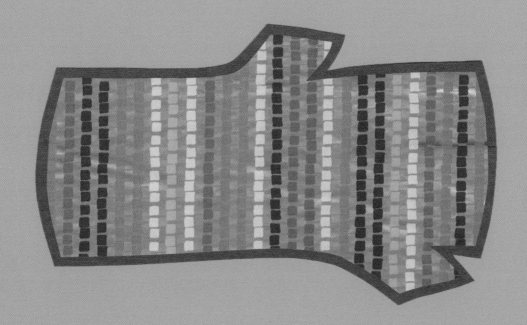

Thus he asked, "Why do you see the speck in another's eye, when you have a log in your own?"

He also shared many parables, short stories with hidden meanings.

But even when he spelled

things out in simple terms,

many people misunderstood

his message.

He said that

only a few seeds

find good soil

and grow.

And he declared that

it was better

to save

one lost sheep

than to care

only for the ones who were already safely with their flock.

He explained to his disciples that the good seeds were those who had heard the news of the kingdom of  heaven and understood it,

and the lost sheep was the solitary

sinner who was more precious

than those who had already

been saved.

But even the disciples

did not always have ears to hear.

When they panicked one night

in a storm at sea, Jesus calmed the waves ...

but not without questioning where their faith had gone.

There were more incredible events, which happened on a grand scale, like when Jesus fed up to 5,000 people with just two fish and five loaves of bread.

Now the Pharisees were the Jewish leaders who kept the holy laws up to date.

But they sometimes missed the purpose of the law and insisted it be followed even if it meant people might be hurt or excluded.

So they did not like it when Jesus worked on the Sabbath by plucking grain and healing people.

Nor did they approve of him staying with tax collectors and saying he forgave other well-known sinners.

The Pharisees took great offense at the kindness Jesus
showed to strangers.

When a Roman soldier begged
Jesus to heal his beloved slave,
Jesus promptly answered
his prayer.

On another occasion Jesus spoke of a certain Samaritan.
Samaritans worshipped the same God as the Jews but were
no longer included in the house of Israel.

Jesus considered this Samaritan to
be a model of faith because

he had cared for a man who had been
robbed, beaten, and left for dead.
The Pharisees began to feel that Jesus was up to no good.

Trouble in Jerusalem

Knowing that people wanted to destroy him, Jesus warned his disciples that his time on earth was coming to an end.

But he promised to come again.

So they found a colt to carry him from the Mount of Olives to Jerusalem to celebrate the Passover.

As he approached the city, people laid branches and clothes on the ground

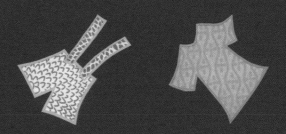

to create a path for him. And they shouted, "Blessed is the king who comes in the name of the Lord!"

When he arrived at the Temple, he toppled the tables of those who were changing money and selling pigeons for sacrifices.

It was right to pay taxes, rendering unto Caesar what was due to him, but inexcusable to turn a house of prayer into a place for profit.

The Sadducees were priestly aristocrats who did not like the Pharisees. They asked what right Jesus had to disrupt the way things were.

They posed trick questions about the resurrection of the dead. But Jesus was very wise with his answers.

And he warned his disciples to beware of self-important scribes who made a show of their long prayers.

On the first night of Passover, Jesus and his disciples
ate their last meal together. He blessed the bread and
offered it in remembrance of his body.

Then he gave thanks for the wine, which he said
was poured for them to celebrate the new bond with God
that would come as a result of his death.

Jesus also predicted that one of his disciples
would betray him -- an idea that was
incomprehensible to them.

After dinner, he went with some of them to the
Garden of Gethsemane at the foot of the Mount of Olives
to spend the night in prayer.

Judas Iscariot meanwhile had made a deal
with some of the new Herod's soldiers.

For thirty pieces of silver,
he led them to Gethsemane
and, with a kiss to his cheek,
identified Jesus for arrest.

Jesus surrendered to the soldiers
and told his disciples not to fight back.

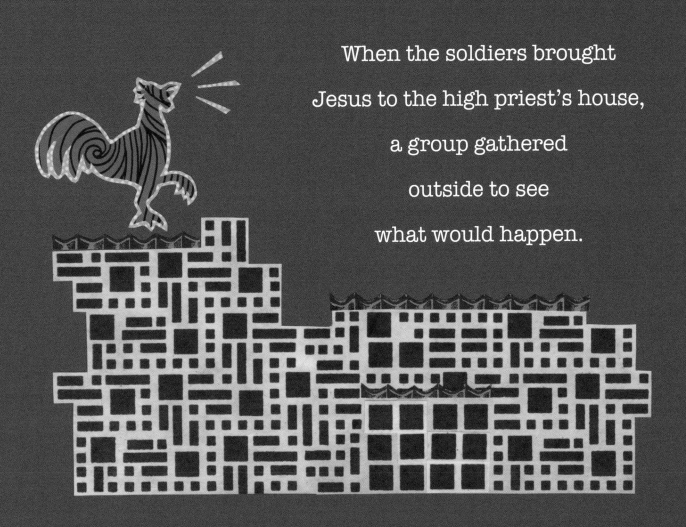

When the soldiers brought
Jesus to the high priest's house,
a group gathered
outside to see
what would happen.

Not wanting to be questioned for being a disciple,
Peter told three different people that he did not know Jesus.

And then he wept,
because he could not believe
he had been too weak to show
his devotion to his teacher.

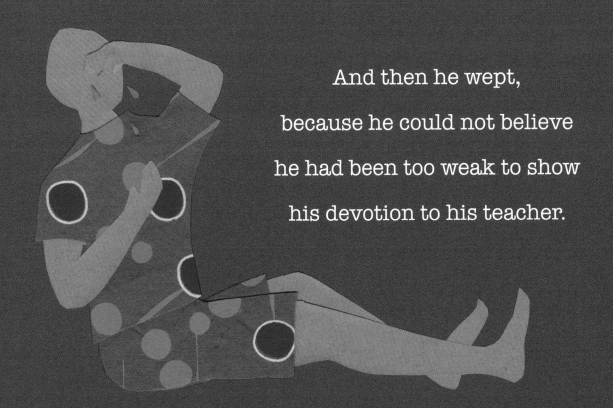

Jesus was then put on trial. Dishonest witnesses condemned him,
but their lies did not add up.
When questioned directly,

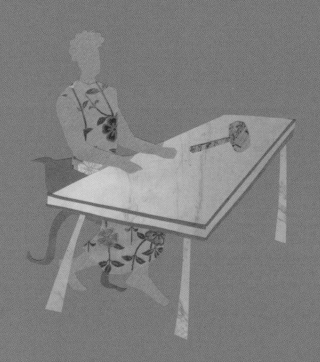

Jesus failed to deny that he was the Son of God.

So they sent him to Pilate,

the Roman governor of Judea,

to have him killed.

Pilate's men whipped Jesus

and mocked him by

crowning him with thorns

and dressing him like a royal

in a purple robe.

Pilate had not found Jesus
guilty of any crime.
He thought the people
might want a notorious robber
and murderer
named Barabbas kept
imprisoned instead.

Out of fear that Caesar
would punish them for saving
a man many called
the king of the Jews, they
sent Jesus to be crucified.

As Jesus was led away, a large crowd followed,
with many women crying for him.

A visitor from

northern Africa,

Simon of Cyrene, was captured
and commanded to carry the cross behind Jesus.

When they arrived at Golgotha, the place of the skull,

the Roman soldiers nailed Jesus to a cross.

They continued

to torment him.

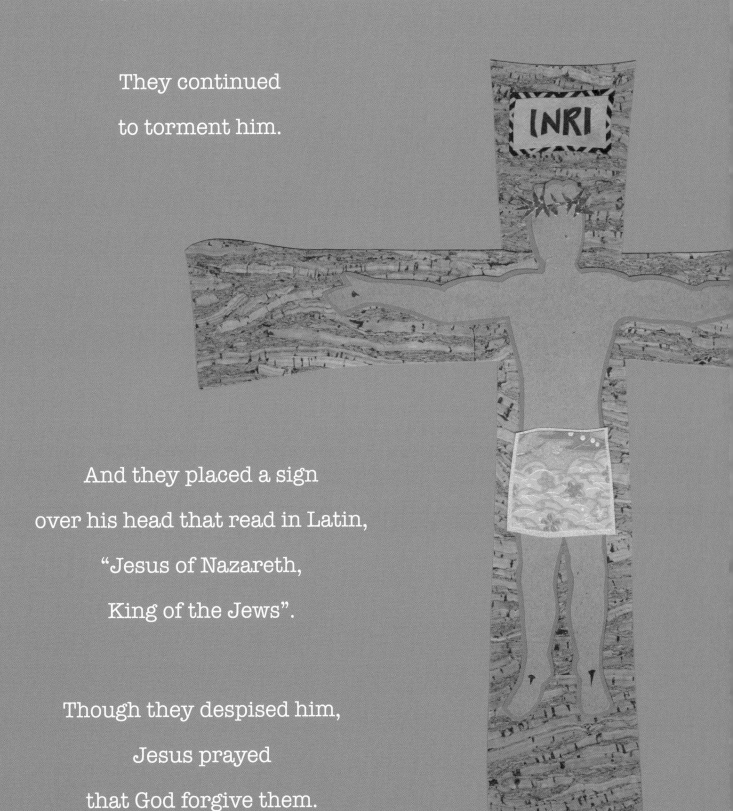

And they placed a sign

over his head that read in Latin,

"Jesus of Nazareth,

King of the Jews".

Though they despised him,

Jesus prayed

that God forgive them.

Jesus hung crucified between two criminals.

One of them asked why, if he was the Son of God, did he not save himself?

But the other man knew that Jesus did not deserve to die and begged that Jesus remember him when he entered God's kingdom.

To this man,
Jesus gave his promise,

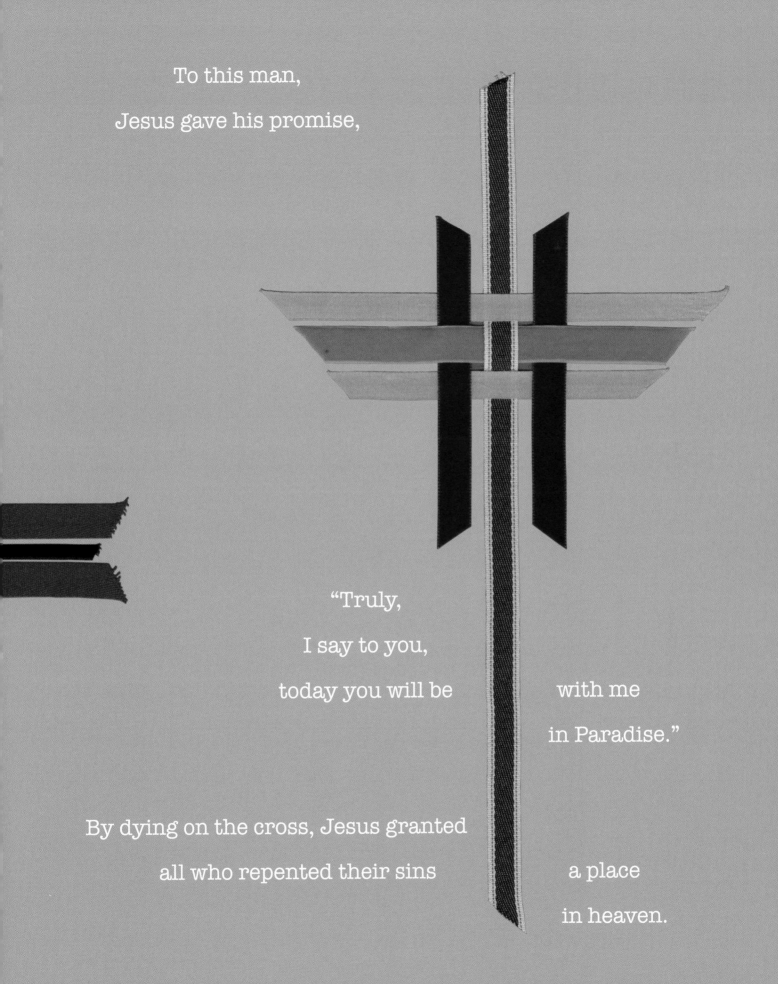

"Truly,
I say to you,
today you will be
with me
in Paradise."

By dying on the cross, Jesus granted
all who repented their sins
a place
in heaven.

This is how he saved the world.

After hours of darkness had passed, Jesus thought
that God might have abandoned him.
Parched with thirst, he was given vinegar to drink.

At last he cried out,
"Father, into your hands
I commit my spirit."
And he died.

INRI

At this moment,
the curtain in the Temple
ripped in two
and the earth quaked.

While his mother Mary and many other women mourned him,
a Jewish councilman named Joseph of Arimathea received
permission from Pilate to wrap the body of Jesus in linen
and place it in a tomb.

They laid Jesus
to rest on the
night of
the Sabbath.

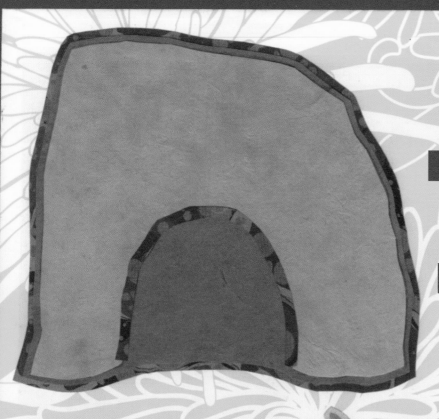

Three days after Jesus died, Mary Magdalene and a few of the other women came to pay their respects at his grave.

They were astonished to find the stone of the tomb rolled away and the body gone.

But some angels informed them that Jesus indeed lived on, just as he had promised.

When the women
told the remaining
disciples
what they had seen,
not everyone
believed them.

Later that day two disciples were walking to a town called Emmaus,
when Jesus appeared
before them.

Not knowing
who he was,
they listened
as he explained
all of the things in the Scriptures that had to do with him.

Only later, when they were breaking bread,

did these two disciples recognize Jesus.

He visited again in Jerusalem to explain the group's mission

to make disciples of all nations,

'I am with you always'

baptizing in the name of the Father, the Son and the Holy Spirit.

Having done these things, Jesus ascended into heaven.

Acts and explanations

A lot would happen before Jesus would come again.

On a day called Pentecost, the Holy Spirit descended

upon everyone who had accepted Jesus as their savior.

Suddenly they began speaking about God in foreign languages

they did not normally know. This wonder proved that the whole

world would witness Jesus as the Lord and Christ.

Three thousand people were baptized on Pentecost.
As Peter and the disciples began healing people
and performing other miraculous acts,

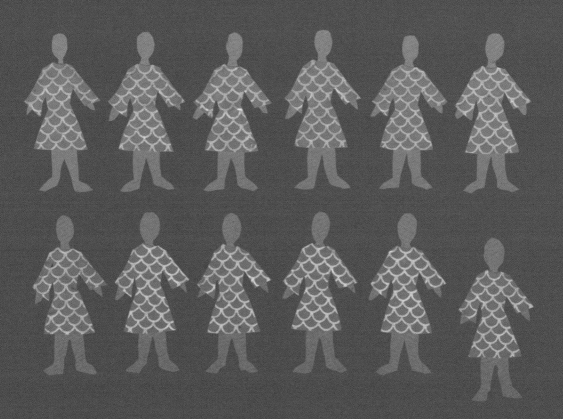

thousands more

came to accept

the news that Jesus

had saved the world

from sin.

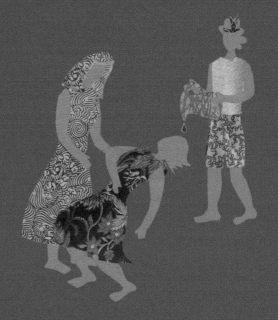

To the traditional leaders in Jerusalem,

this was an outrage.

The disciples blessed a man named Stephen,
who was brought before the religious council for saying
that Jesus had changed life on earth for good.

When Stephen
compared them to
people who had rejected
prophets in the past,
they had him
stoned to death.

Thus Stephen became the first martyr
to die for his faith in Jesus.

Sometime after this,

a voice from heaven told Peter

that he could now eat foods that

had been considered unclean.

And he was sent to the house

of the Gentile Cornelius to do so.

In this way, the Holy Spirit

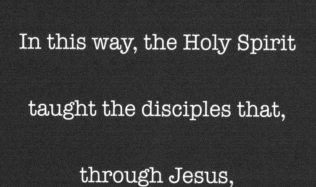

taught the disciples that,

through Jesus,

God had made all things clean.

Even Gentiles could find

repentance and eternal life.

Now Saul was a Jewish policeman and Pharisee who sent many men and women to prison for believing in Jesus.

But on his way to Damascus a light from heaven blinded him, and the voice of Jesus asked, "Why do you persecute me?"

In that moment, Saul became a servant of the Lord, spending the rest of his life proving that Jesus was the Christ.

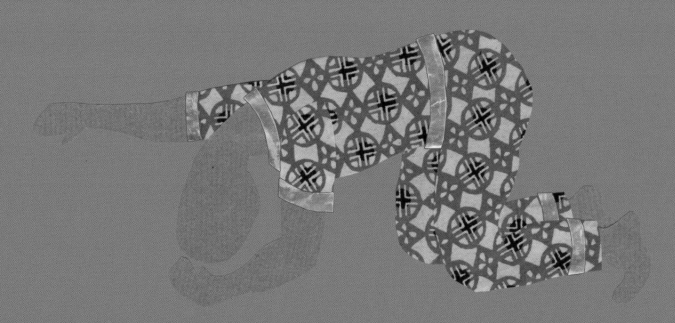

As the most shocking convert of his day,
Saul became a prime target for his old employers.

Over time, he changed his name to Paul and was tortured,

beaten and put into prison twice.

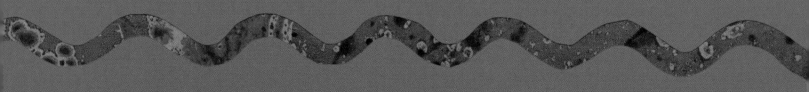

But God's angels and earthquakes helped him to escape.

Paul did not let fear of the law prevent him from traveling across the ancient world to spread the good news about Jesus.

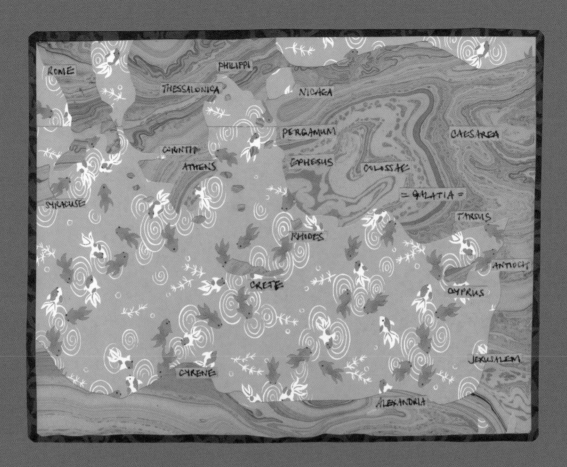

He made many friends in far-away places
and wrote letters to encourage them in the ways of faith.

He sent such epistles to his friends Timothy, Titus and Philemon and to the churches in Corinth, Colossae, Ephesus, Galatia, Philippi, Thessalonica and Rome.

To the Corinthians, who were squabbling amongst themselves, he wrote that love does not mean getting one's way.

He instructed the Philippians not to be selfish and the Colossians and Ephesians to be humble, compassionate, forgiving and kind.

The Galatians and Romans were told not to be slaves to their old ways but freed through the Spirit of the law, which is love.

And to the Thessalonians he promised that no matter what hardships they might suffer, the love of Christ would strengthen and protect them.

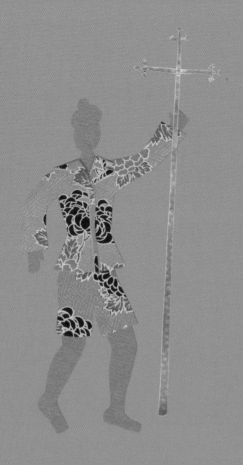

A letter addressed to the Hebrews informed them that they no longer needed to be afraid of dying.

Because Jesus suffered and did not give in to temptation,

he brought a new covenant between God and the world that helps us not to be slaves to sin and death.

Through love and good works, all can receive eternal life.

As an eyewitness to Christ's majesty, the disciple Peter wrote with some equally important advice.

The Lord does not want us merely to follow our instincts or to train our hearts in greed, like animals in a feeding frenzy.

Rather, a tender heart and a humble mind provide the key to a Godly life and the door to the heavenly kingdom.

Other disciples used poetic images to inspire the early members of the Church.

James described the loss of the rich man's possessions after he dies as grass that withers in the sun.

Jude compared

those

who look

only

after

themselves

to waterless

clouds --

and to wandering stars that fade into darkness.

Then John, the author of the fourth gospel,

wrote a letter informing us that

we walk in God's light when we

walk with no fear and

in fellowship with one another.

But when he was living on the island of Patmos,

he had a spectacular mystical vision

of all that will happen before Jesus comes again.

The mystery to be revealed

First he looked up and saw a figure with seven stars in his hand

surrounded by seven menorahs. This divine being recited

messages for the seven churches in Asia concerning

who would be rewarded with eternal life.

When the doors of heaven opened,

there sat the Almighty creator on a throne.

Twenty-four elders in white bowed before Him,

and four creatures with many eyes sang His praises.

Then a Lamb with seven eyes
and seven horns
took a scroll from
the Almighty's right hand.

One by one the Lamb removed the seven seals on the scroll,
and there were four horsemen,
great earthquakes,
falling stars,

and the saving
of servants.

With the seventh seal
came seven angels
to erase the earth and let the heavenly kingdom begin.

And so a battle began to rage in heaven.

The angel Michael and his team slew a ferocious dragon and threw his body to what remained of the earth.

Two beasts soon rose up from the sea and up from the ground, indicating that Satan was fighting back.

But with the Son of Man and an army of millions, the Lamb triumphed over these as well, so that there were no beasts left to worship.

Finally the souls of those who had died for Jesus arose,
and a new Jerusalem came down from heaven,
radiant as a bride on her wedding day.

God was making all things new

and wiping every tear from every eye.

There would no longer be any death – only the water of life.
Jesus, the Lamb, had saved the world once and for all.
And, behold, he was coming soon.

The news about Jesus remains a mystery to many,
but the simple truth is this: by coming to earth as his own son,
God learned how it feels to be human.

Because Jesus suffered for our sake, we are never alone,
no matter what happens to us.

Jesus performed miracles so that we might have faith in his power to heal and like him be always compassionate.

WE ARE ALL GOD'S CHILDREN

#lovenohate

♥u like a sister

MERCY FOR ALL

Pray for your Foes

When we honor the Commandments and love our neighbors as ourselves,

COMPASSION FOR THOSE BEHIND BARS
— Hebrews 10.34

BROTHER, I FEEL YOU

I WAS A STRANGER AND YOU LET ME IN
--Matthew 25:35

NO HATE NO FEAR

FEED THE HUNGRY!

BLESSED ARE YOU WHEN OTHERS CONDEMN YOU Luke 6.22

Sheep without shepherds welcome here.

we follow Jesus and become closer to God.

Jesus turned our worldly expectations on their heads.
Through him the sick are healed, the poor become rich,
and the weak are made strong.

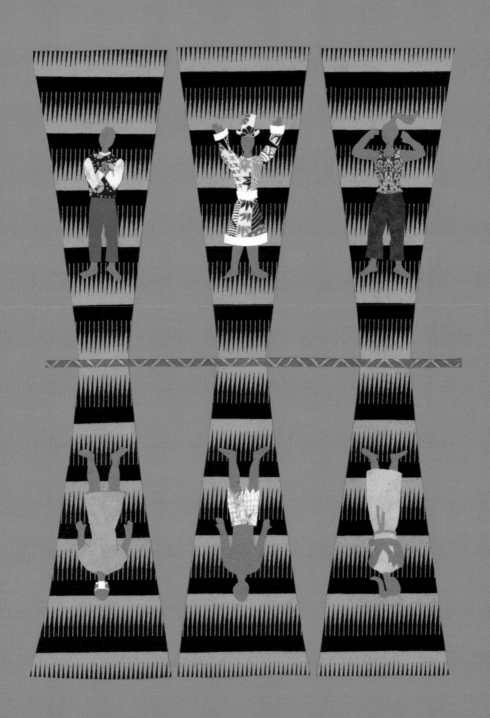

His love helps us not to judge others but to make peace with
them, despite our differences. This is how we live the Word of
God and allow the love of Christ to free us from death.

And this is how the glory of the Lord and the Spirit of heaven
come to life on earth every day.

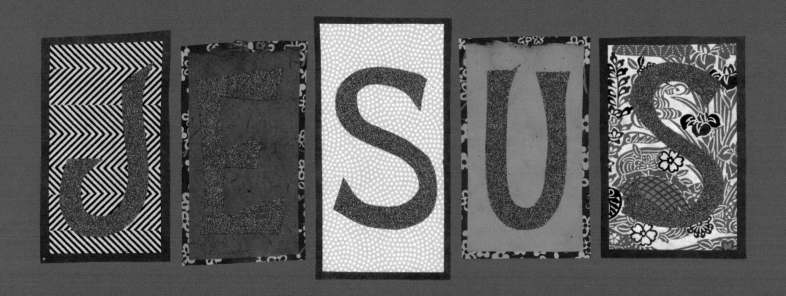

Christians will all agree:

this is extremely wonderful, utterly joyful,

awe-inspiring news indeed.

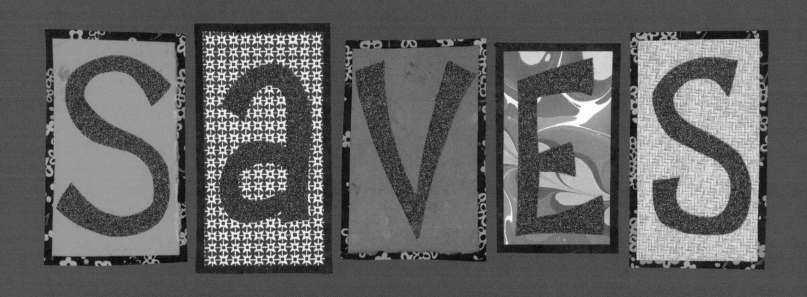

Hallelujah and

Amen!

The fine print

The New Testament consists of four gospels that celebrate the life and resurrection of Jesus, one book detailing the Acts of the Apostles, twenty-one letters or "epistles" about living in the spirit of Christ, and the Book of Revelation. These were written 30-60 years after Jesus died and reflect how a message that originated in the Jewish faith became a gift to the whole world. *"Bullseye" pattern (p.1) from iōta, by C.R. Gibson; ship's hull (p. 4) from Paper Source.*

Matthew and Luke's nativity stories demonstrate that Jesus and John the Baptist fulfilled certain Old Testament prophecies. Where Matthew tells of kings visiting the baby in a house in Bethlehem (2.11-12), Luke shows him lying in a manger, praised by angels and shepherds (2.4-7). The differences between the four gospels suggest decades during which eye witnesses shared stories by word of mouth before others wrote them down. When it came time to decide which writings should be included in the Christian canon, the church fathers recognized that all four accounts were sacred. *Gabriel's garments (pp. 6 and 8) from Caskata Artisanal Papers; luggage (p. 10) by Bella BLVD; "Love Must Have Been" horse and "Smitten" goat (p. 11) from American Crafts; angel's mistletoe from Rossi, Florence.*

For Mark and John, John the Baptist's witness that Jesus would baptize with the Holy Spirit begins the story of his life on earth. In Mark's gospel, the people fail to recognize he is God's son until after his death. In John's, Jesus is the Word of God itself, whose eternal presence allows people to witness grace, truth and light. *Satan's stones are "Em" © Elissa Barbieri for Loop, LLC.*

The fourth chapters of Matthew and Luke's detailed narratives quote Jesus' replies to the devil. Discrepancies between how Matthew, Mark and Luke each describe the call of the disciples and the healing narratives contribute to the theory that there was a further source of stories called Q. The wedding at Cana appears only in John (ch. 2) as a sign that helps the disciples believe in Jesus. *Goldfish (p. 26) by Paper Source; Nathaniel's "Earthtones" by Doodlebug Design, Simon's "Cackle" by SEI, Judas's "Silver Lace" by Pebbles (p. 27); rebirth on "Pluto" by Neisha Crosland (p. 28).*

The Old Testament instruction to love one's neighbor as oneself (Leviticus 19.18) is reiterated in Matthew 22.39, Mark 12.31, and Luke 10.27. This guiding principle of Christianity is frequently ignored when the rich fail to share with the poor and judgment obstructs people from compassion. The centurion and Samaritan stories illustrate that those who are not like us can be models of love and faith. *Camel threads by Egg Press (p. 32).*

39-48  Trouble in Jerusalem
His controversial teachings and prediction that the Temple would be destroyed caused the leaders to conspire against Jesus. Rather than create a community in which all were cared for, the rich and the powerful had used the law to build walls. Jesus' only "crime" was to show that religious practice had become a hypocrisy. Although Luke's disciples tend to stand by Jesus throughout his trial, abandonment by those closest to him occurs in all four gospels. *Backgammon table (p. 40) by OCD for Penny Kennedy; Sadducees are regal in Snow & Graham (p. 41); cock crows (p. 45) and Pilate proposes Barabbas (p. 47) in a detail from aLoveSupreme, South Africa.*

49-56  The most important event of all time
The cross symbolizes the intersection of the divine and earthly realms. But death by crucifixion was no abstract affair. The central Christian paradox is that this gruesome method of execution allowed Jesus to be enthroned as Christ. With criminals on either side of him, the promise of Paradise (Luke 23:43) sprang up among those whom the world most despised -- not as the result of conservative adherence to religious laws. A soldier pierces his side after he dies in John 19.34. The evangelists differ on which women discovered the empty tomb: in Matthew 28.1, Mark 16.1, and Luke 24.10, it is Mary Magdalene and various others; while in John, it is Mary Magdalene alone (20.1-18). *Resurrection chrysanthemum background is © elūm Designs, Inc. (p. 54).*

57-68  Acts and explanations
The Acts of the Apostles is a sequel to Luke and relates the tribulations of the first Christians. Tongues of fire bring the Pentecostal miracle to life in Acts 2. The letter "A" (p. 57) is shown, clockwise from top, in Ugaritic, sign, Arabic, Aramaic, Greek, Japanese, Latin/Roman, Hindi, Hebrew, and Chinese. The epistles address the new nature of faith, the meaning of salvation, and how Jewish Christians and Gentiles could worship together. God prepares the heavenly gift for the descendants of Abraham in Hebrews 11.16, while in John's first letter God is light (1.5) and a love without fear (4.16-18).

The mystery to be revealed

69-76 The author of the Book of Revelation (*apokalypsis* in Greek) may be different from the John who wrote the gospel and the letters. Like Daniel in the Old Testament, John of Patmos presents characters and events that have hidden meanings. The seven-headed beast, for instance, is an allegory for Roman rule. John's resistance literature reveals that the days of the merciless and of those who practice falsehood are numbered. But through the light of Christ, nations shall heal (22.2) -- and death, pain and mourning shall be no more (21.4). *Shweshwe fabric from DaGama, South Africa.*